REHABILITATED FOR LIFE

SMALL BUSINESS FINANCE COURSE

Rehabilitated For Life Publishing Company
Copyright © 2018 RFL

All rights reserved. No part of this publication may be reproduced or transmitted in any form or by any means, including informational storage and retrieval systems, without permission in writing from the copyright holder, except for brief quotations in a review

OUR MISSION

It is our mission to educate communities by building financial literacy programs to provide everyday people with an opportunity to achieve financial independency and business success.

WORKSHOPS

- Advantages and Disadvantages of Business Ownership
- Questions to Consider When Deciding on Starting a Business
- Checklist to Get Your Business Started
- Business entities
- Components of a Business Plan
- Access to Capital

WWW.REHAB4LIFE180.COM

FACT OR FICTION?

- You will have more freedom owning your own business.
- You will be able to choose what you do when you get up in the morning.
- Increased flexibility.
- Need ambition to succeed.
- Entrepreneurs are born not made.
- Anyone can start a business – it's all luck or guts.
- Entrepreneurs are gamblers.
- You need a lot of money to be an entrepreneur.

Fast facts

- A new business is born every 11 seconds in the United States.
- In a study on influential Americans – the defining issue of the 21st Century: Entrepreneurship!
- One in 12 Americans is actively involved in trying to start a new business.

OWNING A BUSINESS

PROS
- Create your own destiny
- Make a difference
- Reach your full potential
- Reap unlimited profits
- Contribute to society and be recognized for your efforts
- Do what you enjoy and have fun at it

CONS
- Uncertainty of income
- Risk of losing your entire investment
- Long hours and hard work
- Lower quality of life until the business gets established
- High levels of stress
- Complete responsibility

ARE YOU ENTREPRENEURIAL MATERIAL?

Entrepreneurs are a special breed of people with varied qualities. They are self-starters, highly motivated, risk-takers and hard workers. Take a few moments at home to complete the following quiz to determine whether you have what it takes to become a business owner.

1. Are you a self-starter? Would characterize yourself as highly motivated? Yes = 5; No = 0
2. Are you a risk taker? Yes=5; No=0
3. Can you get the job done (complete tasks)? Yes=5; No=0
4. Are you disciplined? Yes=5; No=0
5. Are you a hard worker (able to work twelve to fourteen hours per day)? Yes=5; No=0
6. Are you organized? Yes=5; No=0
7. Can you persevere despite the odds? Yes=5; No=0
8. Do you have a good support network (spouse, relatives, friends, etc.)? Yes=5; No=0
9. Are you a problem solver? Yes=5; No=0
10. Are a decision maker? Yes=5; No=0
11. Are you a good communicator? Yes=5; No=0
12. Do you have managing experience? Yes=5; No=0
13. Are you good at record keeping? Yes=5; No=0
14. Can you manage your finances? Yes=5; No=0
15. Do you have enough money saved? Yes=5; No=0

Scoring

50-75- Congrats! You are definitely entrepreneurial material with the right qualities to start and maintain a successful business. This is your time! Go for it!

20-50 – You have a sincere desire to start a business, but need some more work. Fortunately, all business-related skills such as record keeping, managing finances, discipline and risk taking, for example, can be learned. Take relevant classes to help you build upon these skills.

0-20 – You can still fulfill your dream of starting a business. But something is holding you back. Review your answers and ask yourself some hard questions. Remember that despite the results, you can become successful once you dedicate yourself to your dream.

WWW.REHAB4LIFE180.COM

GETTING STARTED?

To start a business you must have motivation, skills and desire. It also takes planning and research.

List the reason why you want to start a business to help you assess whether this is the right decision for you. You must also decide what type of business is right for you based on your experience and skills. Then decide if the business you want to start will fulfill a need in the market. After that you need to plan the how, when and where of starting your business. Use the questions below to evaluate your business idea.

1. Summarize your business idea in 50 words or less. Is this a product or service business, or a combination of both?
2. Where did your business idea come from? (A sudden inspiration, a specific experience, your observations).
3. Is your idea an improvement or variation of an existing product or service? If so, describe why customers will use it instead of what is already available.
4. What is special or unique about what you are offering that will give you an advantage over your competition?
5. List the products or services you plan to sell.
6. Who will own the business? Will it be you or will you have partners?
7. Who will be your major competitors?
8. Is the industry/market for your product or service growing?
9. How much money will you need to start your business? How do you know? And how will you finance the start of your business?
10. Can you make money in your business? Can you charge enough to make a profit?
11. List the top three qualifications you have that will make you likely to succeed in this business?
12. What are your two most important personal goals for the next three years? How does your business fit into these goals?

Notes

CHECKLIST TO GET YOUR BUSINESS STARTED

_____Fictitious Business Name
A declaration by an individual or other business entity stating that they intend to conduct their business under the name they have chosen. A Fictitious Business is the same as a DBA (Doing Business As).

_____Employer Identification Number (EIN)
Can be used to identify a business entity that is legally separate from you. Generally, businesses need an EIN. One exception is a sole-proprietor with no employees. However, sole-proprietors who must pay federal excise or payroll taxes will need an EIN too. If you have employees, you will need to acquire a tax identification number form your state's department of revenue and taxation.

_____Sales and Use Permit (Seller's Permit)
All business selling or leasing tangible property (goods) must obtain a Seller's Permit.

_____Business License and Permits
Required by the city, district, or county in order to begin to operate.

Other items that may be applicable:
- Business Insurance
- Federal Registration of Trademarks and Patents
- Contracts
- Business Lease Agreement
- Documentation of Corporate Filing
- Partnership Agreement

LEGAL ENTITY SELECTION: TYPES OF BUSINESSES

Sole Proprietorship – Business owned by one person

For tax and legal purposes the business is the owner. The unlimited liability factor is probably the greatest disadvantage.

PROS

- Sole owner has total control over the operations of this business.

- Least regulated form of business.

- There are no legal requirements as to how the business must be operated, other than tax records for tax purposes.

- Usually one only need to obtain a license or pay a fee to a local registering authority.

CONS

- All of the personal and business assets of the sole owner are at risk in the sole proprietorship.
- A judgment against the sole proprietorship could reach into personal assess of the sole owner.
- Liability insurance premiums are usually too expensive for the resources of the sole owner.
- It may be difficult to obtain a loan because of the structure. If there is a insufficient collateral, a sole proprietor may have to mortgage a loan or place another piece of personal property as collateral.
- When the sole owner dies, often the business ceases to exist due to the lack of structure in this business form.

Notes

The Limited Partnership – Business owned by two or more people

The limited partnership contains elements of both a traditional partnership and a corporation. The limited partnership may be used when some interested parties want to invest in a partnership but want only limited liability and do not wish to exercise any control over the business activities of the partnership.

The limited partnership is subject to much or regulation on the state level than either the sole proprietorship or regular partnership. Each state has adopted strict regulations according to the Uniform Limited Partnership Act, governing the formation and operation of the limited partnership.

A limited partnership consists of two types of partners: the general partner and the limited partner.

General Partner – One or more people who actively manage the partnership. The general partners are a personal risk for their conduct of the partnership.

Limited Partner – One or more people who invest in the partnership but take no active role in the management of the partnership. The limited partner risks only that which he has invested in the partnership.

PROS

- The limited partner, as long as he remains passive, has no personal liability and risks only that which he invests.

- This type of partnership makes it easier to find investors because of the low risk for the limited partner and the fact that the limited partner shares in the profits and tax deductions with no duties regarding the active conduct of business may make it easier for the partnership to find investors.

CONS

- There is always a chance for a lack of continuity and clear-cut guidelines amongst the partners concerning who does what and how to conduct business.

- Due to the state regulations, limited partnerships are subject to more paperwork than the general partnership.

- General partners maintain full personal risk. The limited partner risks losing the benefits of the limited partner status if they take any active role in the conduct of the activities of the partnership.

The Corporation – Business created by law or under the authority of law

A corporation is an artificial entity created by filing Articles of Incorporation with the Secretary of State. This gives the corporation existence and a legal right to conduct business in the state of incorporation. Corporations are more complex than either a partnership or sole proprietorship and are subject to more regulation by the state. The internal rules of the corporation, which outline the mechanics of the operation and management, are called the by-laws.

Terms pertinent to a corporation
1. Corporate Structure: A concise explanation.
2. Shareholders: They own share in the business but do not engage in the direct management of operations except by electing the directors of the corporation and by voting on major corporate issues.
3. Directors: They can be shareholders, but if they are only Directors. A group known as the Board of Directors is jointly responsible for making the major business decisions for the corporation as well as appointing the officers of the corporation.
4. Officers: They can be shareholders and/or directors, but if they are only officers. They are responsible for the day-to-day operations of the corporate business. Usual titles for the different corporate officers are: President, Vice-president, Secretary and Treasurer.

PROS

- Potential for limited liability is one of the most important advantages of the corporate form of business structure. The liability of corporate debt is generally limited to the amount of money each investor has invested.
- A corporation can theoretically have perpetual existence.
- A shareholder may freely sell, trade or give away his stock unless this right is formally restricted by corporate decision.
- Taxation can be both an advantage and a disadvantage.

CONS

- Due to the organizational structure in a corporation, a certain degree of individual control is lost by incorporation.
- The technical formalities of corporation formation and operation must be strictly observed in order for a business to reap the benefits of corporate existence.
- The initial state fees that must be paid for registration of a corporation can be very high.
- Corporations are also subject to a greater level of governmental regulation than any other type of business.
- Profits are subject to double taxation when distributed to shareholders in the

The Limited Liability Company (LLC)

A Limited Liability Company (LLC) is a hybrid business entity, designed to combine the advantages of a corporation with the tax advantages of a partnership. Like a corporation, the owners of an LLC are not personally liable for the LLC's debts and obligations. Like a partnership, an LLC can be treated as a pass-through entity for tax purposes. Beginning in 1997 the IRS no longer taxes these entities as corporations. They permit the LLC to elect whether taxation as a partnership, sole proprietorship or corporation best fits the needs of its business and its members. This may be advantageous for those who cannot meet the IRS requirements for an "S" corporation and desire the tax pass-through treatment.

What is a Business Plan?

It is a complete written plan describing your business. It covers every facet from buying a pencil to choosing a location. It also includes financial calculations and projections that are critical for the success of a business.

Why write a business plan?

- To sell yourself on the business and evaluate your skills
- For strategic planning and evaluation
- To obtain bank financing for a new business or expansion
- To arrange cooperative or strategic alliances to help you start or expand your business
- To obtain large contracts to secure sales income
- To attract key employees and/or partners
- To motivate and focus your management team
- To gauge growth and resolve problems

Components of a Business Plan?

Cover Letter

Identifies the purpose of the business plan. If it is for financing purposes and it should include the amount of financing being requested, the terms and timing of the financing, and the structure of the financial return being offered.

Executive Summary

The main objective of the Executive Summary is to outline the why and "the what" of the business; what the main objective of the business is. What is the purpose of the business? This is a one to three page highlight of key ideas/plans for your business. The summary should entice the reader and spark interest in the business concept. Your Executive Summary should be written last although it is the first section in your document.

    A. Objective (specific purpose of the plan)
    B. Mission Statement
    C. Who is your customer?
    D. What are your customer's issues or needs?
    E. Customer's solutions

F. Your solution

Description of Business

Should provide a brief history of the business. It includes the business name, how the business is structured, who are the owners, how long it has been organized, and what accomplishments have been achieved to date.

A. Ownership
B. Business entity
C. Company history or your background
D. Products
E. Facilities and location

Description of Products and Services

Explain the services or products your company sells. Refer briefly to the needs being met by your business and how those needs are eing met, key product benefits, and most important customer segments. Describes patents, copyrights and legal and technical considerations. Pricing can also be discussed in this section.

A. Describe product
B. Features and Comparisons
C. Brochures and Specs
D. Costing and Sourcing
E. Technology

Marketing Analysis

The making plan should include a review of industry conditions, a precise definition of the target markets, an analysis of competitor advantages and weaknesses and a plan for promoting and selling your product or service.

Describe the state-of-affairs within your industry segment. What industry is your business representing, what are the industry conditions, how does the business enter the industry.

In this section write a clear description of your target market. Include their needs and wants. Your product/service should offer a solution to the target market or provide a benefit to your customer.

Identify competitors providing the same or similar solution to your target market. For each provide strengths and weaknesses and in conclusion define how you will position your business to compete in the market.

A. What industry are you in?
B. Competition
C. Industry Trends
D. Target Maker Segmentation

E. Who are your customers?

Business Strategy and Operating Procedures

Define how you will get your product or services to your target market. This includes marketing avenues such as advertising, promotions, public relations, and distributing channels. How will you reach customers? How do your target customers make buying decisions? Where do target customers shop for products or services? How will you incorporate a variety of marketing efforts?

How will you measure the success of advertising and promotion effort? Where is your business located? Is the location of your business important? Does your business require special zoning, land or building improvements to accommodate your operation? If location is important, what are the features of your location? If you are creating a product or if you depend on subcontractors to deliver a service, you should know how to contact these sources. In this section you will list your critical suppliers and subcontractors. Briefly describe what material or services are required to complete production. Where do you get your raw materials? How do you find potential suppliers or subcontractors?

A. Marketing Strategy
B. Pricing Strategy
C. Promotion Strategy
D. Distribution Strategy
E. Sales Strategy
F. Strategic Alliance

Management

It is important to know what resources you have in-house to support your business development and growth and what resources you will need to find. You should demonstrate that your management team has technical abilities, marketing abilities and business acumen to succeed. In addition, identify directors and advisors who you will consult with.

A. Prepare an Organization Chart
B. Who is the management team?

Financial Plan

This section should include past financials and future projections based on sound and reasonable assumptions. If the business plan is being presented for financing, the source and use of funds should be defined here.

A. Financial Requirements
B. Capital equipment and supply list
C. Balance sheet
D. Breakeven Analysis
E. Pro-forma income projections (Profit & Loss Statement)

F. Pro-forma Cash Flow

Supporting Documents

A. Tax returns of principals for the last three years
B. Personal financial statement (all banks have these forms)
C. For franchised businesses, a copy of the franchise contract and all supporting documents provided by the franchise
D. Copy of proposed leases or purchase agreement for building space
E. Copy of licenses and other legal documents
F. Copy of resumes of all principals
G. Copies of Letters of Intent from suppliers, etc.

ACCESS TO CAPITAL

It is important to plan how much capital it will take to launch or expand your business. Make your personal financial statement, a start-up expense list, and projections for the business. Once you do your financial planning, it will allow you to analyze whether you need additional funds to successfully start or expand your business.

Capital: What do you need if for?
- Buying supplies and inventory while waiting to get paid
- Paying payroll and rent
- Buying equipment and fixtures
- Buying the business (i.e., franchising)
- Purchasing commercial property

Seep Capital: Seed capital is the money you need to do your initial research and planning for your business.

Start-Up Capital: Start-up, or working capital, is the funding that will help you pay for equipment, rent, supplies, etc., for the first year or so of operation.

Mezzanine (expansion) capital: Mezzanine capital is also known as expansion capital, and it is funding to help your company grow to the next level, purchase bigger and better equipment, or move to a larger facility.

Bride Capital: Bridge funding, as its name implies, bridges the gap between your current financing and the next level of financing.

A Budget will indicate:
- The cash required for necessary labor and/or materials
- Total start-up costs
- Day-to-day maintenance costs
- Revenues needed of support business operations
- Expected profit

The Basic Concepts

The three main elements of a budget are:
- Sales revenue
- Total costs
- Profit

Home Exercise:

To start a business it's best to know what expenses will be needed for at least the first 6 months. At home, answer the following based on the business you intent to start.

Part 1. List the starting Fixed Costs you have to pay only once, such as the following:

$_____ Furniture, fixtures, & equipment.
$_____ Decorating and remodeling
$_____ Installation of fixtures and equipment
$_____ Starting Inventory
$_____ Deposits with public utilities
$_____ Legal and other professional fees
$_____ Licenses and permits
$_____ Advertising and opening promotion
$_____ Advance on lease
$_____ Other and miscellaneous cash requirements

(Add each dollar amount and write total)

Part 2. Now list the estimated monthly expenses, which are Fixed and Variable Costs:

$_____ Salary of owner-manager
$_____ All other salaries and wages
$_____ Payroll taxes and expense
$_____ Rent or lease
$_____ Advertising
$_____ Delivery expense
$_____ Supplies
$_____ Telephone
$_____ Other utilities
$_____ Insurance
$_____ Property Taxes
$_____ Interest expense
$_____ Repairs and maintenance
$_____ Legal and accounting
$_____ Miscellaneous

(Add each dollar amount and write total)

$_____ TOTAL ESTIMATED MONTH EXPENSES

(Multiply by 6 for 6 months and write total)

$_____ Total Estimated Monthly Expenses Multiplied by 6.

TOTAL ESTIMATED CASH NEEDED

Add "Total Estimated Cash to Start" in part one with "Total Estimated Cost multiplied by 6" in Part 2 to get Total Cash Needed

$_____ + $_____

$_____ = TOTAL ESTMIATED CASH NEEDED

_____
_____
_____
_____
_____
_____
_____
_____
_____
_____
_____
_____
_____
_____
_____
_____
_____
_____
_____
_____
_____

Credit

When Financial Institutions review a potential borrower they will look at different categories. Credit score is an important factor for their decision. There are five additional factors that are taken in consideration for a loan evaluation.

The Five C's

Capacity	This is the most important; how will the loan be repaid?
Capital	How much the owner or partners have invested or have at risk.
Collateral	The guarantee that the loan will be repaid.
Conditions	Three fundamentals: General Economics, Geography and Industry.
Character	Some Banks may consider this to be the most important.

Documents That May Be Required By Lenders
- Business tax returns for the past 2 years or personal tax returns for the past 2 years
- Recent paycheck stubs
- Business filings (inclusive of the business)
- Articles of Incorporation (for Corporations)
- Proof of insurance (workers comp/fire/comprehensive/etc.)
- Lease Agreement
- Business Plan (may not be required pending loan amount)
- Recent Personal/business Financial Statement
- Business Bank statements
- Collateral (pending loan amount and credit score)
- Copy of Driver's License and second for of ID (i.e., credit card)
- Statement of what the loan is going to be used for

Note: Some banks may change or have exemptions for start-ups.

General Loan Qualifications

Business owner(s) must:
- Have a business plan
- Be in business for a minimum of 2 years
- Have a strong credit profile
- Inject 15--25% of their own funds.
- Have a profitable business
- Have collateral in the form of either real estate equity, inventory, or contracts
- Have personal and business tax returns
- Have balance sheet and income statements for the business

Note: These are general qualifications. Each bank has specific qualification for their available business loan products and may have exemptions for start-ups.

WWW.REHAB4LIFE180.COM